GERALD O'DRISCOLL (1886–1947) was an Irish sailor, journalist and humourist who also wrote under the pen-name 'Geraldus'. A veteran of the Royal Navy, he wrote several bestselling books memorialising the sailor's world, including *The Musings of a Merry Matloe* (1927) and *Awful Disclosures of a Bluejacket* (1929). *A Dictionary of Naval Slang*, his last book, was published at the height of the Second World War.

RICHARD HUMPHREYS is a British writer and memoirist. Born in Wolverhampton, he spent many years in the Royal Navy as a diver and submariner, including multiple patrols on the UK's Polaris class nuclear submarines in the 1980s. His experiences aboard Britain's nuclear deterrent formed the basis of his bestselling memoir *Under Pressure: Living Life and Avoiding Death on a Nuclear Submarine*, published in 2019. He lives in London.

A

DICTIONARY

—of—

NAVAL SLANG

GERALD O'DRISCOLL

Foreword by Richard Humphreys

Swift

SWIFT PRESS

This edition published by Swift Press, 2021

First published in Great Britain by W.H. Allen, 1943

1 3 5 7 9 10 8 6 4 2

Foreword copyright © Richard Humphreys, 2021

Text design and typesetting by Tetragon, London

A CIP catalogue record for this book is available from the British Library

ISBN: 978-1-80075-393-8
eISBN: 978-1-800-75073-9

A

DICTIONARY
—*of*—
NAVAL SLANG

Foreword

As the rest of the human race settled down to watch Live Aid, a lithe, spotty and nervous teenager gazed out from the Torpoint ferry across the sun-soaked millpond of the River Tamar, wondering what the next twelve weeks had in store. I'd been told by various people to get as fit as possible for both the physical and mental tests that lay ahead; military basic training was going to be a full-on, intensive process.

What nobody had mentioned to me, though, was the trouble I'd have understanding what all the Chief Petty Officers (mostly old salty sea dogs) with years of experience behind them were talking about! Since the days of yore, the Royal Navy has had its own language, or 'Jackspeak', that has, over the last four centuries, come into everyday use for the senior service.

My first introduction to this was on my first day in the RN, when a bespectacled barber and ex-Navy man had shaved my head to within half an inch of its life before shaking my hand and saying, 'Welcome to the Andrew.'

I misunderstood him. 'Hi Andrew, I'm Richard, nice to meet you,' I replied. A torrent of abuse was hurled at me from my left as an enraged Chief Petty Officer with a face the colour of beetroot informed me that 'the Andrew' was actually the term for the Royal Navy. Pusser is another term that can be used to describe the whole of the Navy; it derives from the paymaster and supplies officer of the Navy of old, in other words the bloke who paid you. I still got paid cash in hand when I first joined—the Pusser would deliver the cash into my left hand as I saluted and failed to remember my service number, which I had to shout back at him at the same time.

There are conflicting reports as to the origin of the term 'the Andrew'. Some say it derived from the Christian names of two notorious press-gangers from the Napoleonic and the Age of Sail eras. The most likely explanation, however (and one which O'Driscoll subscribes to), is that the first edible rations on the Royal Navy men-of-war were supplied by a company run by one Andrew Miller, who had such a monopoly on supplies that in many ways he owned the Navy. The phrase stuck.

The rest of my time in basic training I was referred to as a Nozzer, which was a term given to new sailors until they passed out. The term came from an old instructor from some years past who had been well endowed in the nose department!

At the start of my service, we were given a lecture about the perils of too much alcohol and what it can do to the brain and indeed the body. The term 'grand slam' was used to describe the moment the sailor arrived back from a night out on shore, lost control of his bodily functions (the three sphincters), fell asleep (usually with a lit cigarette) and—well, you can imagine the rest! Talking of cigarettes, it was here in basic training that I had my first induction into smoking a Blue Liner. This, believe it or not, was the Navy's own brand of cigarette, strong enough to make a human throat bleed with just one inhalation—it put me off smoking for a long, long time. Phased out by 1991, it must have immediately cut emphysema cases by half. Basic training also involves a trip to the Fang Ferrier–the dentist. My trip involved a return visit and my own version of the film *Marathon Man* with a sadist who put in a filling without anaesthetic and berated me for having the audacity to complain about it.

With basic training behind me, I joined the completely terrifying, baffling, exciting and sometimes monotonous world of submarine warfare. Different to any other branch of the military, the submarine service is thus home to some of the most coarse and ingenious phrases in the Royal Navy. Here are some of my favourites.

angles and dangles   High-speed changes of depth whilst also using large angles of trim. I was terrified when I was first subjected to this whilst on operations. The captain makes sure the foreplanes and the afterplanes are working correctly by tilting the bow up and down fifteen to twenty times, sending the boat hurtling this way and that. It's like being in a fast elevator that moves sideways and backwards as well as up and down! Angles and dangles are used mainly to make sure everything is stowed away and won't bang about if you have to take evasive action—in our case, we needed to be particularly alert to Soviet submarines on Cold War hunter patrol. The chefs used to dread this in case they'd failed to lash down all their pots and pans correctly, which could be a loud and bruising experience.

beer tokens   Money. What else does it need to be called?

bellfin   Stinking and/or sweaty; the inside of a submarine most of the time, especially when submerged for more than a week.

black lighting   Term used when a submarine is at periscope depth at night-time, curtains drawn, minimal red lighting—you can't see anything. But the skipper's in his element on the periscope (or 'peep stick'). Always farcical if there was a watch change in the middle of it, which did happen occasionally. I saw a young sailor trip through one of the blackout curtains and wrap it round the captain accidentally while he was still on the periscope; the effing and jeffing which followed was priceless.

bomber   Polaris/Trident submarine.

bubble   Best to describe it as a spirit level (clinometer) that the planesman uses to keep the boat level in the water, particularly prevalent whilst at periscope depth. The Captain doesn't want his periscope dipping in and out of the water whilst carrying out all-round looks. Some planesmen have been on the receiving end of some almighty bollockings when this occurred.

bunch of bastards   Usually a line of rope that has become entangled and is a nightmare to source either end. Can result in a seaman becoming entangled in the submarine casing and tripping overboard, which looks funny but is potentially very dangerous.

coffin dream   The bunk on a submarine is about the size of a generous bookshelf; it's tiny! About sixty centimetres in width, sixty to seventy centimetres in height and about 1.8 metres in length, it is enclosed on all three sides by a curtain which is then pulled across for total darkness. It feels like something out of a Stephen King novel. If you're at all claustrophobic, submarines are not for you. The bunk is sometimes referred to as the coffin; I used to have two or three coffin dreams per patrol, quite scary nightmares of the sides closing in or the feeling of waking up whilst being buried alive.

crumb brusher   The officers' steward.

Deeps   Nickname of any submariner whose name is not known; our version of 'mate'.

dit   A story, any story.

dogs   The name given to watches between 16.00 and 20.00, split into two separate watches, the first dog and last dog. This is done so the watch roster is equalised.

fire, flood and famine   Exercises that are carried out on pre-patrol work to test the readiness of the crew. A royal pain in the arse.

fish   Torpedoes.

front c*** Anyone who does not keep a watch from AMS [Auxiliary Machinery Space] 2 back to the motor room.

Jimmy First Lieutenant, second in command who has passed the perisher submarine commander training course. In charge of the warfare teams.

kettle The nuclear reactor, so called as it works in a similar way, generating steam by the splitting of atoms in the nuclear reactor, which releases energy as heat. This heat is then used to create high-pressure steam. This steam then generates the power to turn the turbines and propellor, operate life systems (oxygen and fresh water production) and enough power to drive all the electrical systems on board. A nuclear reactor can generate enough output to power a town the size of Swindon!

on the step The truly majestic sight of a nuclear submarine on the surface at full tilt riding the bow wave. This was an incredible experience. Part of my job was as the Navigator's yeoman, so I would sit up top on the bridge watching the boat below. It would be heaving effortlessly through the seas off the glorious west coast of Scotland, sometimes with dolphins bow-riding in the pressure wave created by the boat.

Part Three   The term given to the lowest of the low, the oxygen thief, the unqualified submariner battling away doing eighteen-hour days to qualify and pass sea training to earn the much-sought-after Gold Dolphin badge. Everyone has to do this if they are new to submarines, no matter what their rank. Mine was a nightmare: hours in overalls crawling around dank, sweaty engineering spaces looking for valves, switches and various bits of machinery. It usually involved me clanking my head on low-hanging pipes and forgetting everything within twenty-four hours so I'd have to repeat it. It was all worth it though when you get the old dolphins from the captain and become a fully-fledged submariner—'sun-dodgers', as we're referred to by the rest of the Navy.

pavement pizza   The finest description of the full vomit in Christendom.

scram   When the rods in the reactor are lowered quickly to shut down the reactor.

Sherwood Forest   Name given to the missile compartment of first the Polaris and then the Trident submarines, each of which carried explosive power many times greater than all the bombs dropped in the Second World War. There's a sobering thought. The missile tubes fill the submarine like an apocalyptic orchard.

Skimmers   The name given to the surface fleet by submariners.

sneaky   A covert intelligence trip. For us, this usually involved dropping special forces soldiers from the SBS (the Navy equivalent of the SAS) near land or hunter-killer Cold War excursions against Soviet naval bases or submarines.

snorting both diesels   Snoring.

Teacher   The head of the perisher course designed to find the next generation of submarine captains; the course has a 25% failure rate.

terror shake   I got a few of these on my first patrol when I couldn't get out of my rack (bed) in time to go on watch!

trim   The angle and buoyancy of the submarine; to be in neutral buoyancy and horizontal is the desired result (to 'catch a trim'), not a bow-down angle of twenty degrees plummeting to the ocean floor.

yodel in a bucket   Being seasick. The worst feeling in the world—second only to a Matt Hancock press briefing.

NAVAL SLANG FOR FOODIES

Life on board one of the Navy's underwater boats relies heavily on food, both for morale and for remembering what day of the week it is, as certain food gets served depending on what day of the week it is, e.g. Friday fish and chips, Saturday steak night, Sunday roast dinner and pizza in the evening – you get my drift? There's plenty of lingo about food and drink; here are a few gems.

Action Man pillows   Ravioli (genius).

babies' heads   Steak and kidney pudding from a tin. I'm gagging even now.

ballerina s**t   Pink blancmange or Angel Delight.

cackleberry   Boiled egg.

cheesy hammy eggy   Toast with ham, grated cheese and a fried egg on top, a breakfast staple.

chicken-on-a-raft   Egg on toast.

clacker   Pie crust.

dead fly biscuits   Dried biscuits with fruit in them.

elephant's footprints, Nellie's wellies   Spam fritters. Only to be eaten in the Navy, nowhere else, ever.

fat pill   Bread roll.

harbour cotters   Breaded/battered fish.

jock roast   Minced beef.

Nelson's blood   Rum.

Norman   Chicken.

oggies   Cornish pasties.

potmess   Messdeck 'stew', origin unknown.

ring stinger   Hot curry.

scran   All food. Derived from the old rations (sultanas, currants, raisins and nuts) that supplemented sailors' diets.

scran spanners   Knife and fork. Can also be used as a weapon against annoying shipmates.

seggies   Tinned grapefruit for breakfast. A healthy option compared to the full English that was on offer seven days a week.

s**t-on-a-raft   Kidneys on fried bread. Served for breakfast, usually with a defibrillator close by.

slide   Butter.

sneeze   Pepper.

snorkers   Sausages. Derived from 19th-century dialect for piglet.

Texas strawberries   Baked beans.

tinned fishies   Sardines.

train smash   Tinned tomatoes.

wet   Drink, always tea.

The author Gerald O'Driscoll's long and esteemed service was in the first part of the twentieth century. Serving on ships that would still dominate naval warfare for two decades more until the pre-eminence of submarine warfare from the Second World War onwards. An Irishman born in Cork in 1887, he joined the Royal Navy as a boy and had a long and successful career. He served during the First World War on H.M.S. *Temeraire*, which saw action at the Battle of Jutland. I'll leave him to explain the ins and outs of general naval slang far better than I ever could. This wise Irish sailor spent many a dog watch compiling the dictionary, so crack open a red grenade, have some nine o'clockers, and enjoy this A–Z of lower deck lingo...

RICHARD HUMPHREYS
London, July 2021

A

abaft the screen   The quarter-deck. Might be considered the opposite of 'before the mast'. The region reserved for officers; the glamour of the wardroom environment. The steel casing that usually divides the quarter-deck from the ship's waist is called the screen. Synonymous with **the Q**.

above-board   Honourable, upright.

Abyssinia   A valedictory; so long; farewell. The expression came into favour as a mark of sympathy with the Ethiopians when the Italians invaded their country. It was cheerfully adopted because of its phonetic similarity to 'I'll be seeing you.'

Acid Drops   Synonymous with **Aggs (Agony Column)**, **Bitter Weed, Caustic, Clanking Irons, Famous Crimes** and **Smile Awhile**.

acting green   Pretending to be innocent; assuming to be unacquainted with matters *sub judice*.

admiralty rain   A pessimistic view of the weather. The weather is considered to favour the Admiralty when it gives sunshine during working hours and rain during the **dog watches**, or during any part of one's own time.

adrift   Late, behindhand or unable to keep pace with the routine of the day. Applying to shore leave, the term signifies exceeding the time one is allotted liberty. A delinquent six hours late is declared to 'come off six hours adrift'.

afters   Delicacies to follow; dessert.

Aggie Westons; Aggies   The Royal Sailors' Rest in any of the three famous naval ports—Portsmouth, Devonport and Chatham—founded by the late Dame Agnes E. Weston.

Aggs   (Agony Column) Nickname awarded to all who persistently grumble. 'Old Aggs', however, is the most common sobriquet of the querulous. Synonymous with **Acid Drops, Bitter Weed, Clanking Irons, Famous Crimes** and **Smile Awhile**.

all about   Highly efficient; clever.

Andrew Miller   The alpha and omega of the Royal Navy. Even in the 1870s this name substituted for the Service. One often said, 'When I joined the Andrew'—meaning, of course, the Navy. When more edible rations, particularly soft bread, made their welcome appearance on board of men-of-war, the firm of Andrew Miller had the biggest contract. Andrew Miller was also the name of a notorious press-gang leader of Nelson's day, but his activities have no connection (as some people believe) with the Service.

answer the bugle   At breakfast time (usually) every morning certain men were, and still are, warned to 'answer the bugle' that day. This means attending the defaulters' table (at which the commander usually presides) either as a requestman seeking favourable consideration (such as a half-day's leave) or as a defaulter, where the offender must explain why and wherefore he breaketh the law.

astonicky   Any instrument of corporal punishment. The derivation has been credited to certain Irish ratings whose schoolmaster, they remembered, had a marked weakness for high-faluting language, even to the extent of dubbing his cane 'astonicky'.

B

backing and filling A term seldom used these days except by hoary-headed pensioners. It implied indecision, hesitancy, etc. A person who could not readily make his mind up was described as 'backing and filling'. *Etymology:* A sailing ship passing through a narrow channel was piloted by the trimming of her sails, which alternately moved her ahead and astern. The process was called backing and filling.

bake Implies frustration, a sore disappointment, the failure of a scheme, or unfavourable results. The term springs from a dinner withdrawn from the oven, proving to be the crude and unlovely 'bake' instead of the more savoury roast.

ball 'em off Means simply having a sleep. 'Ball 'em off' hails from the once very frequent job of unravelling a skein of spun yarn or cod-line and rolling it up into a ball. Synonymous with **catchum killala** and **get the head down**.

bandmaster   A pig's head.

Bandy   Not necessarily a bow-legged individual, but any member of the Royal Marine Band.

bare Navy   Tragic memory of Edwardian days when butter or even margarine was a luxury. 'Living on bare Navy' symbolised having to exist on the coarse fare supplied by the Service. It was experienced on long cruises on pre-refrigerator days (up to 1907), when the ship's canteen ran out of the more edible viands. Hard biscuit and tinned beef were the two foremost delicacies of 'bare Navy'.

barrack ranger   Any rating who is reputed to enjoy a long sojourn in a naval barracks is so-called because he dodges the rigours of life afloat.

Barracky   Nickname for the barrack-master. He is usually a shipwright-lieutenant under whose charge the artisan staff in the depot work. Under him come all the barrack repairs as well as the responsibility of a large number of stores. He is the only officer allotted a private house in barrack territory.

bash; basher   Synonymous with **winger**; 'basher' is a corruption of 'masher'.

batchy   (i) Synonymous with **wet, crackers** and **loopy**.

(ii) A nickname usually applied to a renowned devil-may-care. From 'bats in the belfry'.

beach   Terra firma, needless to say. Your matloe enjoys being poetical at times and refers to a trip ashore as 'going on the beach'—or a **beacher**.

beacher   As stated above, a trip ashore. 'Beacher, Harry?' testifies to the value of economy in words, for it asks Harry in two words if he is going ashore. Synonymous with **on the beach**.

beating up   Sly negotiations in order to curry favour with superiors. 'Lashing out' as soon as officers (particularly the commander) heave into sight. The term is borrowed from the lingo of boat-sailing, i.e. so to move the helm as to take every possible advantage the wind may offer.

bender   A story, a yarn, e.g. 'spin a bender'.

bird   All ornithological labels usually apply to the misfits of the Navy; persons who are troublesome, who cannot be trusted to perform a job of work or remain at their places of duty. The allusion refers to their ability to fall asleep and remain so, even if standing on one leg. Synonymous with **crow**, **fowl** and **pelican**.

birthday   A man is said to have had a birthday when he has imbibed not wisely but too well. In the old days when naval men were more fraternal, sympathetic consideration was accorded to anyone obliged to spend his birthday on board ship, and the birthday celebrant was the recipient of many tots or of any **gash** (ii) rum as a form of felicitation. In some messes a wise caterer kept a list of his messmates' 'birthdays' in order to ensure that they had only one each year.

Bitter Weed   Synonymous with **Acid Drops**, **Aggs (Agony Column)**, **Bitter Weed**, **Clanking Irons**, **Famous Crimes** and **Smile Awhile**.

blackguard's pension The minimum of long-service pensions granted to naval men. A man who misconducts himself to such an extent that, at the expiration of his time, he cannot boast of even one good-conduct badge, must atone for his past by being granted a very meagre pension indeed. Before 1915 it was as little as 9/- a week; it is now in the neighbourhood of 19/- and some odd coppers.

black-outs   Wrens' knickers; Wrens' knickers are black (so the author is informed), hence 'black-outs'. The lingo hails from the Wrens themselves—not from matloes.

Blitz   A bore; a nuisance; a pest.

blitzed   In the past tense, defeated, impotent, drunk or incapable. Needless to explain what dulcet lingo this weed sprouted from. Synonymous with **tin-hats**, **canned**, **half rats**, **scats**, **shot away**, **well oiled**, etc.

bloke   When preceded by the definite article, 'bloke' indicates any person in authority. 'The Bloke', however, is usually the commander or medical officer of the ship.

Blondie   Any effeminate-looking youth who sports very fair hair must not be offended if he should be hailed as 'Blondie'.

blow   To boast a good deal. From 'blowing one's trumpet'.

Blue Peter   The long-service and good-conduct silver medal awarded to naval ratings after 15 years' continuous good service. It carries with it the well-merited gratuity of £20. A facetious allusion to this award is that it was nobly earned for 15 years' undiscovered crime.

Bombay oyster   A restorative for those who have gazed upon the wine when it was crimson. It consists of an egg beaten into a quarter-glass of vinegar and well sprinkled with pepper and salt. As a tonic this is reputed to have powerful healing properties—but the author hesitates to substantiate this statement.

bottle   A sharp reprimand, a scolding. To be the recipient of a 'bottle' or a 'drink' means being found fault with. The abstract 'bottle' is represented as containing a liquid uncommonly strong, and certainly more tolerable when kept securely corked.

bottle it up   To hold one's temper for a future occasion; to repress emotions; to hold a grievance in memory with a view to reprisals. The analogy is a 'rum' one. Certain naval ratings who have the fortune to draw the neat rum ration may prefer to put it in a bottle instead of drinking it at the time of issue—usually 11 a.m. The beverage proves more suitable for many at a late hour.

bring out   To introduce to the limelight. More commonly used in reference to sport, particularly boxing. 'Tucker Brown brought him out' (coached him). Again, one who has trained a noted singer is said to have 'brought him out'.

bring up with a round turn   To 'bring up with a round turn', 'choke one's luff' or 'bring one to his bearings' signifies taking the conceit out of a person by having so much the better of him in an argument or a quarrel as to render him powerless to proceed further. It may also imply a direct order to keep silent or take the consequences.

broadside   An apt retort; an epigram so potent as to **sink** an opponent. A broadside or **salvo** is a number of guns fired simultaneously; scoring a hit, of course, the effect would be very much more dynamic than that of only one gun finding the target.

Brocky   The sobriquet of anyone who sports a rough or pimply complexion.

browned off   Has many meanings and hails from the Army. Defeated, cheated, outdone, imposed upon or punished. 'I've been browned off for a quid'; 'I browned him off at crib'; 'the skipper browned him off with seven days' leave stopped.'

bubbly   The rum ration issued daily. Sometimes it is referred to as 'Navy'. 'It cost me a week's Navy to get that sub'—meaning that the speaker managed to get a sub, the price being a tot every day for a week. Synonymous with **mutiny**.

buckshee   From the Persian *baksheesh*. Something for nothing; extra; free, gratis; additional to the usual allowance.

buffer   Usually 'chief buffer'. A senior or chief petty officer under whose administration the work on the upper deck is carried out. He is the commander's right-hand man.

Bugs   Synonymous with **Chats** (ii), **Crabby**.

Bug-whiskers   A derisive salutation to the owner of an untidy or badly grown beard.

bullock   Any member of the Royal Marines. A tradition of the Royal Marines is that its members always go straight at a person and never around him, even if more convenient, hence 'bullock'. A marine is always addressed familiarly as 'Royal' and never as Joe or **Joey**, as so many misguided writers declare. Synonymous with **leatherneck** and **turkey**.

Bunt; Bunting   The cognomens of any signal rating. A signalman is a bunting-tosser. The term applies to the material of which the flags are made.

buzz   A rumour. 'What's the buzz?' 'Have you heard the latest buzz?'

C

cabin   A euphemism for cell punishment; i.e. 'ten days' cabin'.

caboose   Synonymous with **dicky**.

Callao   A sort of El Dorado existence. A ship is said to be 'Callao' when living conditions, routine, food, officers and shipmates are highly favourable. *Etymology*: Sacred to cherished memories of the Peruvian seaport where, once upon a time, bacchanalian orgies were the order of the day.

camel corps   Towards the close of the 19th century it was a common sight in the home ports to see a young seaman or stoker struggling home beneath the weight of a great white bag of dirty clothes, hammocks, etc. The burden was his shipmates' washing, and he was taking it to his wife. There were no separation or children's allowances in those days, and the young married couple who faced life on 1/7 to 2/- a day had to resort to the labour of the wash-tub in order to pay the rent for one room and make ends meet. The late Mr Lionel Yexley, founder and editor of *The Fleet*, wrote a very distressing picture of this struggle, as he himself had bitter experience of it.

canned   Synonymous with **tin-hats, blitzed, half rats, scats, shot away, well oiled,** etc.

capribbon pint   Refers to the froth formed from beer or stout on top of an inadequately filled pint measure; a very **shaky** pint. In pre-First World War days the staff in the wet canteens of naval barracks worked hand-in-hand with the **Crushers**, with one titanic aim—to rob the bluejacket customers. In exchange for his twopence, 'Jack' was handed a very **shaky** and unwholesome-looking pint. If he grumbled about the issue, he was immediately ejected by the patrol at the **Crusher**'s order and threatened by the tyrant with a charge of insubordination. Truly did those black marketeers of the wet canteen and some shady ships' police enrich themselves brazenly at 'Jack's' expense.

C.D.   Popular abbreviation for 'Captain's Discretion'. In cases involving the captain's consideration, whether it be awards, rewards, favours or punishments, when he is not bounded or inhibited by certain clauses and regulations, the liberty of meting out judgment as he thinks fit is popularly called C.D. The same letters in the bad old days had a far more sinister interpretation—*Crown Debt*, the aftermath of a spell in prison. Though the erring matloe had expiated his offence, he found himself heavily in debt on returning to civilisation. This was to be expected as, having had no pay in prison, his wages could only count from the date of his release. But then he had to foot the bill by paying the railway fares of the escort who conducted him to prison, to say nothing of the heavy fine that may have found its way into the charge sheet. To add to his misery, he was forced to wear a garb of shame, a heavy coarse canvas suit with the letters C.D. surmounted by a stigmatising broad arrow.

cargo shifter A one-time derisive reference to any Royal Naval Reserve officer. The expression has happily died down, possibly because the Navy has discovered how highly efficient an R.N.R. officer can be... it has taken a world war to discover it. The nickname now is **Rocky**, which applies to any type of reserve rating.

35

carry round   A man is said to be 'carried around the ship' when he has to be shown everything in connection with his duties and when his work has very often to be done for him. The implication is that he is as helpless as a baby and so has to be 'carried round'.

catch a crab   A man is said to 'catch a crab' when, through erratic feathering, the blade of his oar is jammed beneath the water, the loom catches him across the chest and he is in danger of being knocked off the thwart.

catch the boat   To 'catch the boat' implies punctuality for any event, whether it be for a meal, a smoke, the theatre, or the liberty boat for shore. Obversely, to 'miss the boat' signifies being late. 'The boat's shoved off' may mean that there is no more tea in the urn or eatables in the dish.

catchum killala   Synonymous with **ball 'em off** and **get the head down**.

Caustic   Synonymous with **Acid Drops, Aggs (Agony Column), Bitter Weed, Clanking Irons, Famous Crimes** and **Smile Awhile**.

chance his arm   To 'chance one's arm' means to take a bold risk in any undertaking. The relevance of the term implies that when a man 'chances his arm' he risks being disrated; he chances losing the decorations on his arm.

Charley More   The synonym for everything that is upright, honest and reasonable. As long ago as 1840 a Maltese publican of that name had a huge sign-board over his pub on which was flamboyantly inscribed CHARLEY MORE THE FAIR THING. The panegyric caught the eyes of naval men so often that Charley More was accepted into their vocabulary as the very pinnacle of altruism and integrity. 'Come on, act Charley More' was often a very earnest appeal to a man's sense of fair play.

Chats   (i) Short for Chatham, the Eastern seaport.
(ii) The uneuphonious sobriquet applied to anyone who is habitually untidy, or **chatty**. Synonymous with **Bugs**.

chatty   Dirty, grubby. From Chatham, the entrance to which was never very picturesque.

Chef   All members of the cooks' branch to-day are deservedly hailed as 'Chef'. At one time the sobriquets were **Greasy-Neck** and **Sloshy**, but happily these have faded into oblivion, for the modern cook is worthy of high esteem. See **cook of the mess, cook of the rook** and **in the house**.

Chemist   The ship's surgeon.

chew fat   A man is said to chew (or chaw) his fat when he talks a lot; in other words, make quite extravagant movements with his mouth. In the old days, the fat of the salt pork was so inedible that in most cases it could only be chewed. So when a poor sailor was chewing his fat he was certainly giving his mouth a good deal of exercise.

Chimp   Synonymous with **Doggo** and **Tarzan**.

chippy; chippy-chap   Any member of the shipwright branch. A shipwright is usually addressed as 'Chippy'. From chips—chips of wood, shavings.

chitted up   Getting in touch with any rating by application to the head of his department. In a big place like the R.N. barracks, or indeed in any of our big warships, it is not always easy to locate an individual who may be required. By application to the head of his department the man may be quickly traced; in a case of urgency he may be broadcast for. This is called 'chitting up' a person.

chocker   Fed up; disgusted; have endured to the limit; won't stand any more. Derived from the seamanship term 'chock-a-block', which indicates that if the two blocks of a purchase are hauled close together (two blocks), no further power can be obtained from that purchase.

chuck his hand in   A tragic proceeding. A man who refuses to perform his duty or who stoutly disobeys an order to carry on with his usual work is said to 'chuck his hand in'. He is then put under arrest (**down below**) and, not infrequently, imprisonment follows. *Etymology*: A card game. The player, seeing that his hand of cards is hopeless to achieve any points, throws the cards on the table with disgust—he chucks his hand in.

chucking-up boat   Signifies aiding and abetting. A chucking-up boat's crew is really a crowd of enthusiastic supporters who form a boat's crew of their own and follow in the wake of their shipmates' racing crews, cheering them to the echo and encouraging them all the way.

chummy ship   Portrays one of the Navy's most fascinating traditions. By some mysterious, almost psychic, means, the crews of two ships in a fleet or squadron become endeared to each other. A comradeship that baffles sentiment endures and the crews of each show an eager readiness to do anything for their compeers in the 'chummy ship'. Meeting on shore, they join in drinking bouts, toast each other's racing crews, walk about arm in arm, wear each other's cap-ribbons, and are ever willing and eager to fight each other's battles in the event of coming to a clash with a rival or **enemy ship**. Racing bouts between the two ships are always noted for their sportsmanlike friendliness. For instance, if the forecastlemen's racing cutter's crew of H.M.S. *A* challenge ditto of H.M.S. *B*, the losing crew invites the victors on board their ship to supper. At the expense of the forecastlemen of the losing ship a top-hole feast is spread, and a smoking concert follows.

Clampy   Nickname for the owner of very large feet. Synonymous with **Flatfoot**.

Clanking Irons Synonymous with **Acid Drops, Aggs (Agony Column), Bitter Weed, Caustic, Famous Crimes** and **Smile Awhile**.

clew up To finish; to terminate. From the lingo of sailing.

clink Synonymous with **rattle**.

clinker-knocker Old name for **dustman**; synonymous with **fireman** and **shovel engineer**.

clobber Clothes, usually those about to be washed.

Clubs A physical training instructor. Usually hailed as 'Clubs', but referred to as a P.T.I. In the old days he was called a tumbler.

Cocoa Boatswain The old name for an instructor of cookery. The implication was in a derisive vein. It is seldom heard to-day, possibly because the Navy has learned that a warrant-officer cook is just as important to the welfare of the Navy as a warrant officer of any other branch.

come up Otherwise number eleven (once 10A) punishment; i.e. seven days' 10A or seven days' come up. In addition to enduring many other unpleasant restrictions and drills, a poor defaulter was not even allowed to eat his meals with his own messmates. Authority decreed he should be treated as a social pariah and, at mealtimes, he had to take his meals on the cold upper deck in company with his guilty brethren. Usually as he ascended the ladder with his meals in his hands he received ironical cheers from his shipmates. Thus 'come up'.

comp   From 'compensation'. Payment in lieu of rations. A comp number: an appointment where one receives an allowance for victualling; very often it is a shore job. There are three stages of comp. These are V.A. (victualling allowance), P.A. (provision allowance), and L.P.A. (lodging and provision allowance). Referred to as 'on comp'.

compo   Compensation, payment, e.g. 'a month's compo'.

confirmed   Promotion in the Navy to-day is what might be termed 'provisional'. A rating, on advancement, adopts the acting rank for a period of twelve months, after which, if found satisfactory, he is 'confirmed' in the rank by his captain.

conk   A nose. A man with a big nose is called 'Conky' or **Trunky**. Even a Wren, so afflicted, has received the same uncharitable nickname from her sisters.

cook of the mess   In all broadside messes in the Service, two men (usually partners or cooking chums) take up culinary duties for 24 or 48 hours. They wash all the crockery, pots and pans, and are mainly responsible for the cleanliness of their mess. They also peel the potatoes and (especially in small ships, where general mess is not the order) even make the dinner for the following day. They do not, however, cook it; that job is left to the ship's cook, who receives it at the galley. 'I'm **in the house** to-day' means that the speaker is cook. Synonymous with **cook of the rook** and **in the house**. See also **chef**.

cook of the rook   Synonymous with **cook of the mess** and **in the house**.

cookum fry   To die, to pass away. The term originally applied to the destination immediately after demise, and the climatic condition thereof is expressed by the verb. No matloe was considered eligible for admission to the beatific region, so 'cookum fry' became identified, rather inevitably, with the other place.

cop   Signifies capture. It is associated with 'copper'; to be copped or winged means apprehended or caught in the act. A person, place or thing is assessed as 'no cop' when weighed in the balance and found wanting. 'That fellow's no cop'—no capture.

corker   A blanket and pillow which have seen better days but still remain very serviceable when a welcome siesta is indicated.

cottage   Synonymous with **rook, domicile** and **drum**.

Crabby   Synonymous with **Bugs**.

crackers   Synonymous with **wet, batchy** (i) and **loopy**.

crack townies   To 'crack townies' or **old ships** with anyone is a diplomatic effort to gain his favour in order to reap material benefit. The claims of 'townies' or **old ships** are considered to have strong sentimental value, and to 'crack' them is considered an unusually gilt-edged investment.

cross bows   To pass in front of one. The term has passed into table etiquette; a man reaching across his neighbour for anything on the table may say, 'Excuse my crossing your bows.'

crow   Synonymous with **bird, fowl** and **pelican**.

Crushers   Regulating petty officers who work under the supervision of the master-at-arms in a ship. They were once known as ship's police, but to-day are officially referred to as R.P.Os. As their job is partly punitive, they are not always held in high esteem. In this, however, they are paying for the sins of their 'fathers', who were the real crushers, body-snatchers and sleuth-hounds of a shady past. These forerunners possessed much power and were noted for their corrupt practices, chief of which were **rabbiting** and taking tips. Their nefarious sobriquet, 'body-snatcher' (recalling the activities of people who dug up dead bodies for gain), is happily not heard to-day. It was associated with the revolting practice of getting men into trouble (lining them up) and then releasing them for a shilling or sixpence. Synonymous with **Gestapo** and **Scotland Yard**.

D

Daddy An affectionate nickname accorded to any captain whose appearance and disposition are benevolent and fatherly; one who gives kindly advice at the defaulter's table. Usually a very popular captain.

Daily Mirror ship A ship which receives much press publicity is usually so-called.

deado Fast asleep.

Derby When there is a vacancy for promotion, all likely candidates are considered to be 'in the Derby'.

dicky A small compartment; a secluded or out-of-the-way corner; small. Synonymous with **caboose**.

dicky-collar The Service blue collar worn by ratings dressed as seamen. Dicky-flannel was a serviceable miniature garment invented by Victorian bluejackets, which it was once death to the law to wear. The old service flannel (of blessed memory), though an excellent garment, was far too heavy in warm weather for many, so, for their greater comfort, they resorted to the dicky-flannel—a very small addition which went over the head, presenting the material's back and front, which were then tied together with white tapes.

dicky run   A quiet and uneventful expedition on shore entailing little expense.

dingbat   A blow.

dip   To suffer loss (figuratively, go down); to disappear suddenly. To be 'dipped' means to be disrated, i.e. be punished by reduction to an inferior rating; to fail in an examination; also to become bottom dog in any financial transaction, e.g. 'I dipped five bob on the spade.'

dish-walloper   Synonymous with **flunkey**.

ditch   The ocean, the sea; the verb 'to ditch' or dump means to heave anything overboard. Synonymous with **pond**.

47

dive-bombers Junior artisan ratings of a Royal Naval barracks who, though they rank with leading rates, are accorded the privilege of messing in the petty officers' mess. The specification was awarded them because of their habit of 'diving' into the soft arm-chairs while their seniors in rank, and certainly elders, remain standing or, if lucky, relegated to less comfortable seats.

dobeying The operation of washing clothes.

dobeying firm A company formed (usually two in number) for the sole purpose of 'making a **pay-day**'. Proclaiming themselves as the Lily-white Firm, they solicit their shipmates to sling along their 'dirties'. These they wash, dry and fold neatly before handing them back to their customers. The usual charge is two-pence apiece, bedcovers, hammocks 1/-, and blankets 1/6. These toilers often amass a very gratifying figure for their labours—but they certainly earn it.

Doc The complimentary nickname of any of the sick berth branch.

dodger A sweeper; a cleaner or caretaker of any com-partment.

dodging Pompey Shirking work; skulking. Origin is said to be associated with the insurgents of Spartacus who, after a heavy defeat, were fleeing from Pompey, the Roman general.

Doggo Uncharitable nickname of all who are cheated of feature by dissembling nature. Synonymous with **Chimp** and **Tarzan**.

dog watch Everyone knows that a dog watch is a space of two hours' duration from 4 p.m. to 6 p.m. and again from 6 p.m. until 8 p.m. In naval lingo, however, 'dog watch' is usually a very exaggerated estimate of a short duration spoken with marked contempt, e.g. 'the Boer War didn't last a dog watch.'

doing a never Skulking; dodging duty or work. Modern definition: helping Hitler.

doing a weep Lamenting; grousing.

domicile Synonymous with **rook, cottage** and **drum**.

doughbash Originally a Chinese washing boy who came on board with the **dobeying** (note combination of **dobey** and **basher**); nag a pet, a favourite; synonymous with **winger**.

down below A man is said to be 'down below' when he has been put under arrest, i.e. isolated and under a sentry's charge. In the old days, offenders were confined in compartments two or three decks below the living quarters.

draft-chit A notice to quit. A naval rating is notified for draft to a ship or shore station through the drafting office of his home port or division. He usually learns of his forthcoming exit a day or two before his long week-end is due.

draw water People who take up a lot of room or whose lumbering movements are molesting others are usually accused of drawing a lot of water. This analogy is, of course, that a ship afloat which displaces only the amount of her own tonnage, on this occasion exceeds the normal amount.

drip A new word for a grouse or a complaint: 'He hasn't half got a drip on, the old barnacle.'

Drip-tin   A pessimist; applies to anyone who continues to harp on the same grievance, 'Old Drip-tin'.

drum   Synonymous with **rook, cottage** and **domicile**.

Duffo   Synonymous with **Westo**.

dummy run   A speedy rehearsal.

Dummy Week   Payment in home waters takes place every second Friday. The week following the no-payment Friday is termed 'Dummy Week' and is usually a very heart-aching period for the insolvent.

dustman   A stoker rating. In the old days he was also known as a **fireman, clinker-knocker** and **shovel engineer**.

E

elephant's part The part of the spectator. One who elects to watch others working and does not make any attempt to lend a hand is said to be doing the 'elephant's part'.

end's-a-wagging An announcement that any movement or transaction is drawing to a close. The idiom is borrowed from the word passed that the end of a rope which is being laboriously hauled along, coiled down or reeled up is at last in sight.

enemy ships Unfortunately, ships may be found in a fleet or squadron which do not hit it off very well. Years ago, this rivalry was painfully symbolised by many disputes and fights on shore. So serious were these clashes at times that leave would not be granted to both ships on the same day or evening.

F

fair wind   Signifies a vacuum; emptiness. When a matloe looks into a milk-jug and finds it empty he declares, 'There's a fair wind in the milk-jug.'

fall out of the boat   A man 'falls out of the boat' if he has been dismissed from a society through a violation of its laws, if he has failed to attend meetings or dances that once attracted him, and also if he has broken the pledge after being a teetotaller.

Famous Crimes   Synonymous with **Acid Drops**, **Aggs (Agony Column)**, **Bitter Weed**, **Caustic**, **Clanking Irons** and **Smile Awhile**.

fanny   The sacred receptacle in which the rum ration is fetched.

Fanny Adams   A name given to a suspicious brand of meat when it first appeared in preserved form at the middle of the 19th century. It was believed to be called 'tinned mutton'. In 1812 the entire country was shocked by the discovery of the body of a young woman in a dreadful state of mutilation. The victim was subsequently identified as one Fanny Adams, but the mystery of her murder apparently remained unsolved since the unsightly remains were so crudely identified with the new brand of preserved meat.

fireman   Old name for **dustman**. Synonymous with **clinker-knocker** and **shovel engineer**.

first and first   Refers to being in the first class for conduct and first class for leave. A man's shore-going leave (which is a privilege) usually depends upon his conduct. A delinquent who commits himself may be relegated to the second class for conduct and therefore second class for leave. In this stage he is permitted to go ashore only once a fortnight. Years ago there was even a third stage for habitual leave-breakers, which was called 'limited leave', or more popularly termed 'limits'. At this stage a poor offender could only go on shore once a quarter.

first turn of the screw   The motto of many insolvents. For a week before ships abroad left a station to return to England, many amusing incidents occurred on board. Elusive and impoverished matloes were to be seen hiding in every nook and corner dodging their creditors—traders, tailors, photographers, etc. Whenever they were asked how they would manage to liquidate their debts, they usually fell back on the callous proverb—'The first turn of the screw [i.e. first revolution of the propellor] pays all debts.'

flag eight   Used amongst signal ratings; a warning that someone in authority is near. Flag eight was the fleet signal for enemy in sight.

flan; flannel   Bounce, bluff and general overtures of being a go-getter, especially if invested with a lot of harangue. The term recalls the empty railings of a wash-deck boatswain who, in the old days, served out flannel for cleaning purposes with a fund of exhortation on the necessity for rigid economy. Hence the analogy 'dealing out the flannel'.

Flannel-foot   An uncompassionate allusion to a victim of bad feet.

flap   To dash about, work briskly, earnestly and ostentatiously to such an extent as to attract attention: 'Come on, flap your wings.' 'Flapping' is synonymous with **lashing out**.

flashing up The act of raising the oil fuel to a temperature high enough to cause a flash when a light is applied. This is usually about 200 deg. F.

Flatfoot A matloe's own nickname for himself. Until 1909 boots were scarcely ever worn on board by seamen. Because of this their feet expanded to an alarming degree, and when they had to don their boots the experience was usually a painful one.

flog To overwork; to exploit; to utilise to an unlimited degree; to read up or study incessantly; (in reference to apparel) to wear almost continuously; also to sell or barter.

flog the cat A term signifying remorse. Sorrow for something done or left undone, e.g. 'I flogged the cat I never passed for the **killick** earlier.' The analogy recalls the ludicrous side of the indiscretion when the victim is prompted to revenge himself upon a poor, inoffensive cat.

flunkey Any member of the officers' steward branch may be so-called. This branch was before 1919 known as officers' servants, and its personnel was enlisted for service usually for a period of five years. After the sitting of the Jerram Committee in 1919, their states advanced with a substantial rise in payment and establishment of continuous service. Synonymous with **dishwalloper**.

flush   Even; at the same level, balanced. A man is said to be 'flush' when he has sufficient money to meet expenses.

flyer   Cute; tactful. The remark 'no flies' on any person is a marked compliment to his shrewdness and adaptability. He is made of better material than that to which flies adhere.

fore and aft rig   Refers to the peak cap and reefer jacket as worn by ratings not dressed as seamen. It is so-called because of its sharp contour in contrast with the 'square-rig' uniform of the ancient seaman, i.e. the sailor serge suit with blue collar.

foreigner   Usually anyone whose home is a long distance from the place or port where his ship or station is at present. 'I'm a foreigner here.' Opposite to **native**.

four by two   More commonly referred to as 'the old four-be-two'—a sort of abstract noun that may refer to anything; a synonym for 'gadget'. Originally, 'four-by-two' was the designation of very serviceable flannelette supplied for the purpose of cleaning the barrels of rifles. It was supplied by the yard and marked off in sections (oblongs) of four inches by two. Each of these sections was cut off and distributed to ratings armed with rifles. The breath of scandal once declared that as a bird is known by its note, so is a chief armourer's wife by her four-by-two petticoat.

fowl   Synonymous with **bird**, **crow** and **pelican**.

Friday while   A 'Friday while' is a long week-end's leave from Friday until Monday. The 'while' is a facetious tilt at the Yorkshireman's substitution of the word for 'until'.

Froggie   Nickname for a Frenchman; not infrequently the cognomen of a Channel Islander. The nickname is a compliment to the Frenchman's reputed partiality for frogs.

G

Gannet The sobriquet of a habitual glutton; one who bolts his food or whose appetite is seldom appeased.

gash (i) To sweep.
(ii) Over and above, surplus. Synonymous with **plussers**.

gashens Refuse, sweepings, debris.

Gate A derisive appellative directed at a loquacious individual, esp. should he not be very popular. (Gate, of course, being a big mouth.)

gate and gaiters In its infancy was a scurrilous taunt applied to the official bearing and bureaucratic ranting of gunners' mates who, in those ancient days, were influenced by a traditional superiority complex—'He's all gate and gaiters.' To-day it applies to any overbearing individual who wears gaiters.

gens A one-time affectionate contraction for general leave, which was a periodical privilege of 24 to 72 hours' liberty. The term has now evolved into 'general quarters'.

Gestapo Applies to the branch of regulating petty officers. Patrols or indeed anyone on police duties are usually referred to as 'the Gestapo'. Synonymous with **Crushers** and **Scotland Yard**.

get away with it A man is said to 'get away with it' if he has escaped punishment for some offence he committed—if he has been pardoned, cautioned, reprimanded or acquitted. The analogy recalls the luck of the fish getting away with the bait.

get the head down Synonymous with **ball 'em off** and **catchum killala**.

get your lugs back In the imperative mood is an unconventional invitation to eat, drink and be merry.

give a miss To give anything a 'miss' is to avoid, ignore or cancel it, as the case may be. If a man changes his mind about going to the theatre, he gives it a miss. To give anybody a miss is to avoid his company. 'Take my tip and give that guy a miss; he's not much **cop**.'

gobbie   A coastguard. Also symbolises a man whose wash-deck duties on board ship are on the quarter-deck.

goffer   A drink of any effervescent quality.

going astern   A man who has absent-mindedly put his cap on back to front is declared to be 'going astern'.

Gold-dust   Almost defunct term for **Paybob** or **Pusser**.

good hand   Synonymous with **taut hand**.

goon   Sometime before the Second World War, because of their raw and somewhat weedy appearance, the youths in training at Exmouth Block, R.N. Barracks, Devonport, were nicknamed 'goons', and Exmouth Block became popular as 'Goon Valley'. The effigy hails from the weird and somewhat attenuated personnel of the Popeye cartoons.

graft   Applies to one's work. A man who is thoroughly acquainted with his work is appraised as 'knowing his graft'—an inestimable virtue in the Navy. Believed to have its origin in naval prisons, where offenders were assigned to work points and grafts in hammock clews and lashings. Seamen usually excelled in this class of work, but other ratings experienced much difficulty and were obliged to submit to instruction which was not too politely ladled out. Hence 'knowing his graft' signifies that a man merits consideration for his proficiency.

Greasy-Neck   Outdated term for **Chef**. Synonymous with **Sloshy**.

green coat   The abstract mantle of pretence. Anyone who simulates being 'green' or innocent is reputed for wearing or shipping the green coat. A persistence in the pretence is colloquialised as buttoning it up: 'He's buttoning up the old green coat again.'

green rub   Unmerited retribution. If a man is punished when it really is not his fault, it is referred to as a 'green rub'.

Gunnery Jack; Guns   The senior gunnery officer of the ship. The 'Jack' was associated with his reputation as a fanatic. Likewise, 'Torpedo Jack' is a synonym for the torpedo officer, but he is more popularly known as the T.L.

gutzkrieg A pain in the stomach. Adapted from the terminology of Cassandra, a hidebound satirist of the *Daily Mirror*.

Guzz The western naval seaport of Plymouth and Devonport. Staddon Point, the loftiest peak noted coming up the Channel, was once known as Guzzle Point.

H

half rats   Synonymous with **tin-hats, blitzed, canned, scats, shot away, well oiled**, etc.

hand-draulic   A satirical corruption of 'hydraulic', which referred to hydraulic machinery. Anything done by manual labour without the aid of electrical or mechanical equipment is facetiously symbolised as being 'hand-draulic'.

Harry Frees; Harry's   Immunity from payment. To be given anything without having to pay for it is to get it 'Harry Frees'. Name associated with an ex-**jaunty** called Freeman, whom the 'troops' nicknamed Harry. He was not very popular.

Harry Tate's   The realm of the ludicrous. Anything presenting a laughable aspect. For instance, if some drill or evolution savoured of one or two flaws or revealed any traces of absurdity it would be termed a 'proper Harry Tate's evolution'.

hatchway nip   Was the iniquitous caper of the **rum-fiend** of years ago. Carrying the **fanny** of rum from the upper deck, he often paused at the top of the hatchway and helped himself to a libation.

haul on   A sinister implication which flavours strongly of blackmail. When a man has a 'haul' on a shipmate, he more or less knows something about that shipmate which it would be extremely disadvantageous to the gentleman if divulged, e.g. 'Young Smithy can say what he likes to **Tommy** the boatswain: I don't mind betting he has a haul on **Tommy**.'

helmet   Any head covering is called a 'helmet'.

hide   Synonymous with **rind** and **skin**.

H.O.   Short for duration of war. Hostilities Only.

hookpot; hooker   A contemptuous reference to any ship. A hookpot was an old tin utensil fitted with hooks for hanging. Though it seldom served a useful purpose, it had to be kept clean and polished. It was happily abolished in 1908.

hookrope party   Delinquents of bygone days. Men who volunteered for any sort of dirty work on the Sabbath morning in order to escape the ordeal of attending divisions. They usually pleaded that they did not have a decent suit to wear or one smart enough to pass the fastidious eye of the captain.

hot   Particular to the extent of being a pet fad. An admiral, for instance, who is reputed to be 'hot on haircuts' may be the cause of a great rush to the ship's barber just before his inspection. A captain who nurses a weakness for chinstays being properly sewn on his charges' caps is said to be 'hot on chinstays'.

hurrah trip   A trip of a squadron or one or two ships around the British Isles in order to popularise the British Navy.

in the house Synonymous with **cook of the mess** and **cook of the rook**. See also **chef**.

J

Jack Dusty Formerly the appellative of a ship's steward assistant; now any member of the supply branch below the rating of supply petty officer. *Etymology*: From the noticeable amount of dust created in the bread-room when the bread was being stowed or tinned, or biscuit distributed, a job at which Jack always had to be present.

Jacker Any native of Cornwall who cannot rid himself of the dialect of that county.

Jack Strop An obstreperous individual, usually in a pot-valiant sense; a poseur of the would-be rough and tough. The term recalls the devil-may-care bacchanalian of the 19th century.

Jago A proper noun that has blossomed into an abstract one. The name of an ex-instructor of cookery who was responsible for much of the messing improvement and victualling systems in the western wing of the Service. He was the pioneer of the general mess movement and worked energetically to promote the comfort of all ratings. In many ships the name Jago is synonymous with the Service itself, i.e. **pussers**. A pair of Service boots is very often referred to as 'a pair of Jagos', and it is believed by many that the name Jago will live longer than that of Nelson.

jam An achievement gained in a game through sheer good luck. A word usually associated with unmerited fortune on a billiard table.

jankers The bugle notes of defaulters.

jaunty The chief of police on board; the supreme head of the regulating staff; the master-at-arms. He is the only chief petty officer who wears a frock coat and sword. From the French *gendarme*. The old French prisoners who were confined in hulks addressed their gaoler as 'gendarme', which when pronounced 'John-dom' impressed the British seaman: thus Johnty, or jaunty.

Jimmy Bungs Is, or rather was, the ship's cooper. He made and repaired bread-barges, tubs and casks but, in

69

general, acted as a sort of aide-de-camp to the supply branch. The rating is now abolished.

Jimmy-the-One   The senior lieutenant-commander of the ship. He is just 'Jimmy', or 'James the First' with the 'troops', and **Number One** amongst the officers.

Joey   The senior marine officer on board. Note: marines are never called Joeys, and certainly not 'jollies'.

Jonas   A corruption of Jonah. Anyone whose presence is suspected of causing disaster or bringing misfortune to others though he himself may come to no harm: 'Who's the Jonas in this blooming watch?'

Juggins   The unfortunate one: the one who **takes the can back**, or shoulders the blame. Believed to be associated with the song, 'I'm Billy Muggins, commonly known as a Juggins.'

jump   Outstrip in the race for promotion. If a rating is promoted before compeers who are actually senior to him on the roster, he is adjudged to have 'jumped' those compeers. On his promotion to the rank of captain, the late Admiral Beatty is stated to have 'jumped' 200 commanders—i.e. jumped over their heads.

K

ki   Cocoa. The Navy's traditional weakness for brevity is often evidenced by referring to items merely by their first letters or syllables. Cocoa became 'kay', which the Cockney twisted to 'ki'.

killick   A leading seaman; the next rank above A.B. (Able Seaman), the anchor worn by leading rates.

L

Lady Godiva bloke A term of derision applied to one who is over-fastidious as to the appearance of his hair, teeth or fingernails.

lap ahead Anything done in advance in order to gain time is referred to as a 'lap ahead'.

lashing out Synonymous with **flapping**.

Leatherneck Any member of the Royal Marines. 'Leatherneck' refers of course to the light leather strap which used to secure one part of a Royal Marine's tunic collar to the other. Synonymous with **Bullock** and **Turkey**.

leg-pulling Everyone knows what is meant by 'He's only pulling your leg,' otherwise codding or aiming to take a rise out of one, but how many know of its origin? Many years ago in London, an elusive type of footpad was highly skilled in the art of tripping people up by dexterously inserting his leg between those of his victims. The fallen man was robbed by accomplices as he lay on the ground. These types of footpad were known to Scotland Yard as 'trippers-up', and the very fact that they pulled the legs of their victims to complete the attack gave rise to the expression so many of us hear to-day.

lift   Elevation, promotion. 'I hear you're getting the lift' is a cheery greeting.

lighthouse   The service pepper-dredger.

line the pencil   To 'line the pencil' for any place expresses the intention of going to that place. The term is derived from the phraseology connected with the late Admiral Sir Percy Scott's dotter.

Lofty   The nickname for a tall person.

long-winded   Late, tardy or, more frequently, a long time working on the one job; likened to a ship a very long time on the one tack.

loopy   Synonymous with **wet**, **batchy** (i) and **crackers**.

lose deal   To suffer loss; to experience a disappointment. (To gain deal, on the other hand, is to experience profitable results. See **windward**.)

lose knees   To fall so violently in love that the emotions generated weaken the knees and rob them of the power to keep vertical. A rather exaggerated simile, but we read of a waiter who, on first beholding the charms of Lady Langtry, collapsed in the midst of a trayful of delicacies. [Emilie 'Lillie' Langtry (née Le Breton; 13 October 1853–12 February 1929) was a 19th-century actress and socialite.]

Lot's wife   Ancient term for the mess's salt-pot.

lush up   To 'lush up' anybody is to treat him—or her.

luftwaffe   An unpleasant odour.

M

Machine, The Systematic inauguration. Ratings joining or rejoining a naval depot pass through divers departments, including passing the doctor and dental surgeon—index, victualling, regulating and divisional offices. The routine of passing from one to the other is so efficiently conducted that the whole process is called 'The Machine'.

madwoman's water Very weak tea

make and mend Really means an afternoon off, or a half-holiday. One of the Navy's traditions is to give a half-day each week for the purpose of making and repairing clothes. On these occasions, the very last thing a naval man gives his attention to is his wardrobe. If he doesn't write a letter, he may produce the **corker** and seek a well-earned rest. Indeed, 'make and mend' has long been a synonym for a siesta.

matloe   A sailor; usually applies to any man dressed as a seaman. From the French *matelot*.

Mick   An Irishman, of course, but also 'mick, a popular contraction for hammock.

Mickey Mouse   The elegant nomenclature which applies to the newly established branch of motor mechanics. The letters M.M. on the arms of these ratings indicate this but also recall, to the humour-loving matloe, Walt Disney's famous creation.

mop   To drink.

mouldy decrepit old vet   Usually a grouser in the winter of his career; a miserable malice not forty years of age who looks sixty and insists on telling the younger fry that he could jump over their heads when he was their age.

muster by the open list (or ledger)   An observance which takes place on board ship at least once a quarter. Originally it was purported to be so the captain should satisfy himself that every name on the ship's ledger for which payment was drawn had a corresponding duplicate of flesh and blood. Ratings assemble for this ceremony (usually in their Sunday best) according to their numbers on the ledger. The captain is seated magisterially at a table. Beside him is his clerk or the chief writer. In rear of him are many of the ship's officers. The writer calls the name of each rating in turn; the captain presides judicially with one eye on the ledger and the other on the man in front of him. As each man's name is called, he takes a pace forward, stands in front of the captain and salutes. (Men dressed as seamen take off their caps with a flourish.) He then answers his payment number. Immediately, and as clearly as possible, he will declare his rating and his non-substantive rating, then any additional qualification for which he receives payment, and lastly the number of good-conduct badges he may possess. The concatenation runs something like this: 'Number three-sixty-one, sir: leading seaman, leading torpedoman, diver first class, two good-conduct badges.' With that he salutes respectfully again (or replaces his headgear), turns right and walks smartly away. Muster by the ledger is also carried out on every occasion of admiral's inspection, after which any rating who so desires may interview the admiral, either to consult him on some private affair or state a grievance.

N

native   As the word implies, one whose home is in the port. One of course becomes a native when ties of friendship, courtship or marriage necessitate his going ashore at every opportunity. Opposite to **foreigner**.

Navvie   The navigating officer. Wardroom officers refer to this learned colleague as 'The Pilot'.

neaters   Otherwise neat rum; a glorious tonic; the monopoly of chief and petty officers.

niggly   Gouging, skimshanking; unscrupulous manoeuvres to gain favouritism; snivelling.

Noo, The   Edinburgh. Obviously the Scottish colloquialism signifying the immediate present (the now) impressed naval men as worthy of a place in their lingo.

north-easter A melancholy term implying economical, rather than meteorological, gravity. North-east on the compass-card is marked N.E., but N.E. also means 'not entitled'—by no means a kindly salutation to a rating answering his call to the pay-table.

number Appointment, job, duty. 'What number have you got?' means 'What is your job?' or 'What duty have you got?' 'A quiet number' means an easy job, a soft billet, and the more the dignity of its office excuses one from the routine work of the ship, the 'quieter' it is.

Number One Of old, the first lieutenant, now the senior lieutenant-commander of the ship. Synonymous with **Jimmy-the-One**.

Nutty The nickname for any person with a large head.

Old Man   (i) An individual who sports marked paternal idiosyncrasies in his attitude towards a shipmate of tenderer years; one who usually takes a fatherly interest in a young fellow and spares no pains to help him on. See **winger**.

(ii) Really speaking, the supreme head of any department. The paymaster-commander, for instance, is **Paybob** to all the crew, but to his own staff he is the Old Man; the senior shipwright officer may be younger than many of his own subordinates, but to them he is the Old Man. Note: in the Merchant Navy the captain is always the Old Man, but this is not the case in the Royal Navy—though his own galley's crew may refer to him as such.

old ship   Otherwise an old shipmate. The term is invested with strong, confraternal sentimentality. The fact of being an old shipmate of anybody's invokes a prior claim for sympathetic consideration on his part—though this tradition is often disputed with the rejoinder, 'Old ships are leaky.' See also **crack townies**.

old soldier 'Don't come the old soldier' is a very frequent rejoinder which implies 'Don't take liberties' or 'Don't put on airs and try to make out you're a big noise.' In the Army the 'old soldier' is a veteran who, by virtue of his age and experience, is credited with having much knowledge and is therefore a very useful arbiter when an argument arises. He is (or was) a person of importance, therefore to pose as the old soldier is a wasted assumption on people who know better.

one-beller A story, an anecdote. The term is a relic of the Victorian era, when garrulous matloes, stimulated by the flowing bowl, exchanged stories. The time of the day would be one bell (12.30 p.m.), just after the rum was issued.

on the beach Synonymous with **beacher**.

open out Go quicker. 'Come on, let's open out!' To increase speed. Applies to opening out the throttle valve more in the engine room.

open up a tin   Here the noun caustic or **strongers** is understood. When an individual 'opens up a tin' he is very indignant and rails abusively, and with a wealth of invective, at the irony of his fate. Of course, those allegorical 'tins' contain many powerful chemicals that, having been '**bottled up** for years' escape with greater violence when the process of opening commences.

Opposition Bill   A derisive nickname accorded to that very unpopular figure who aims to court popularity by pretending that he is well-informed. No matter what anybody says, he will challenge or oppose in the hopes that he will impress his hearers with his sapience. Usually his knowledge is discovered to be so meagre that it is not large enough to convince him how very ignorant he really is.

P

part brass-rags To sever friendship. **Raggie** means a comrade, because in the old days sworn friends kept their cleaning rags in the same bag. If they fell out with each other, one of them removed his rags as a token of his displeasure. 'Parted brass-rags' therefore implies a breaking off of friendly relations.

Paybob The Paymaster. 'Paybob' is to-day the most hackneyed appellative. Synonymous with **Pusser**. See also **Gold-dust**.

pay-day A nest-egg; a comfortable sum of money. To 'make a pay-day' means to labour in order to accumulate wealth.

peg The emblem of the New Leaf. 'I'm going to put the peg in after this week-end'—'I'm not going ashore any more, I'm putting the peg right in.' In most cases, 'putting in the peg' is concerned with turning T.T.

[teetotal] and saving money. When the erring matloe discovers that too much of a good thing confers no lasting benefit he very wisely puts the peg in—for how long is a secret between himself and his Maker?

pelican   Synonymous with **bird**, **crow** and **fowl**.

pennants flying   A matloe declares that his 'pennants are flying' when he overhears, or suspects he hears, others talking about him. A ship wishing to make a signal to another ship hoists that vessel's pennants (i.e. her number). If the ship so hailed is not quick to respond by running up her answering pennant, all other ships in the vicinity may send out a very ironic reminder by hoisting the self-same pennants. So many ships flying her pennants—the subject of general interest: hence the analogy to the overhearing of oneself being spoken about.

perks   Extra work as a punishment. Believed to have originated from the good sense of one Commander Perkins who, noting that little advantage was to be gained in making offenders face the paintwork ('10A punishment'), promptly condemned the corrective as utterly childish and gave the men work to do instead. See also **come up**.

pick up To find fault; to be questioned concerning some flaw or omission. If a man is told by the patrol to button his coat up properly, or appraised by his divisional officer that his hair is much too long, or questioned by the skipper as to where he got that strange collar, he is 'picked up' in each case. The term is derived from the shady past, when matloes were often so hopelessly drunk that they had to be picked up bodily by a patrol and carried to the liberty boat. 'Pick up' also means to meet by appointment: 'I'll pick you up at the Town Hall.' *Etymology*: A ship mooring at a buoy anchorage 'picks up' the buoy.

pier-head jump An immediate **draft-chit**.

pile up points To win favour; to behave in such a manner, under a superior's notice, as to ensure favourable consideration at a later date. See **points**.

playing on To 'play on' anything is to rely upon the official power invested in that same thing. For instance, if a brand-new leading seaman appears to be over-officious, he is said to be 'playing on his something old hook'. The hook (anchor, and symbol of authority) indeed protects him from receiving a severe drubbing.

plussers   Extras; additional. The term speaks for itself. 'Plussers', however, generally applies to the amount of rum remaining in the **fanny** after everyone has had his tot. Synonymous with **gash** (ii).

points   Marks of merit in an examination.

Pompey   Nickname for Portsmouth. The breath of scandal says some old admiral, learning of the loose morals of Portsmouth, declared the town to be more like Pompeii every day.

pond   Synonymous with **ditch**.

Pongo   A soldier.

Poultice-mixer   The old-time uncharitable nickname for any member of the sick berth branch. It has happily died out, and a member of the sick berth branch to-day is hailed by the more academic **Doc**.

Provy   Short for Providence! 'I'll have to trust to Provy.'

prowl   An authority is said to be 'on the prowl' when he is walking round for the sole purpose of finding faults, e.g. 'Look out! Jimmy is on the prowl.'

Pusser Corruption of 'purser'. Synonymous with **Paybob**, but more associated with Service observance. See also **Gold-dust**.

pussers A corruption of 'purser'. A rating is said to be 'pussers' when he rigidly adheres to Service regulations; strict, to the point, conscientious. A man is nicknamed **Pusser** if he wears ready-made or ungainly garments. The ready-made clothes supplied by the purser just before the First World War were anything but picturesque, and rather than wear them the average matloe patronised a naval outfitter to whom he had to pay a far higher price, but he was certainly more respectably clothed. Untidy men of that day received the sobriquet **Pusser**.

Pusser's dagger; Pusser's dirk The service knife with spike issued to seamen ratings; a very useful implement. It was once a very important part of a seaman's kit; indeed, it was death to the law for any such rating not to have one in his possession whilst a member of a boat's crew. The modern knife is a very elaborate implement and can be deftly used either as a screw-driver or a tin opener.

Pusser's dip   The Service candle; it sheds a good light and burns steadily for eight hours.

Pusser's tally   A fictitious name; an alias shamelessly adopted by erring gondoliers and readily surrendered to the gullible. The pursers of the early part of the 19th century were often as unscrupulous a lot of rogues as are any of the brazen racketeers who run the black markets to-day. Their books were well stocked with names of naval ratings who certainly did not exist, and they lined their pockets with the money they received as pay for these fictitious ratings. From this system of fraud sprang the ritual **muster by the open list**.

pull his weight   This term has even passed into journalism. A man is said to 'pull his weight' when he performs, at least, what is expected from him, nothing more and nothing less. The expression hails from boat-racing and referred to one of a crew who does not contribute any extra effort to the struggle beyond that of 'pulling his own weight'.

put in   'I put in to see the comm,' otherwise 'I put in a request to see the commander.' Most favours, privileges, claims, etc. are officially dealt with through the ritual of an interview with the commander. This is engineered by a written request signed by the rating's divisional officer. At 'commander's requestmen' the following day the petitioner sees the comm, and states his case. If the comm approves, he says 'granted!' If he disapproves, the order is short and sweet—'not granted!'—and the **jaunty** repeats it in case the applicant should have any lingering doubt. Important requests (such as those involving money, promotion, allotments, etc.) are dealt with by the captain. If a rating has any family trouble which he does not wish to disclose in the presence of others, he may request to 'see the captain privately', whence every consideration will be accorded him. To-day, minor requests may be dealt with by a divisional officer.

Putty   The ship's painter; the nickname of every painter.

Q

the Q   Synonymous with **abaft the screen**.

R

rabbit Any article of Government property smuggled on shore is called a 'rabbit'. *Etymology*: The breath of scandal says that many years ago sailors used to catch rabbits at Trevol Range [Trevol Rifle Ranges is a military facility in Cornwall, near Torpoint] for the purpose of making them a present to someone ashore. No policeman at the dockyard gates investigated the rabbit until one, becoming suspicious, had a closer peek. The 'rabbit' he saw in the hands of a brazen delinquent was nothing more than a rabbit's head over a pound perique of tobacco. So 'rabbit' became popular after that.

raggie A comrade, a chum. In the old days, men who were firm friends kept their brightwork rags in the same bag. Each knew his own rags, so there was no diving for the best and no quarrels for possession. See **part brass-rags**.

ranko   A queue; to 'pick up ranko' is to take one's place in a queue.

rattle   The Assizes, the defaulters' table, the seat of justice on board ship where one must face the music for violation of the law. To 'score a rattle' means being entered on the report-sheet to answer a charge the following day. Synonymous with **clink**.

red lead   Fried tomatoes, usually those from a tin.

relief   A successor; one who replaces another in a ship is usually his 'relief'. From the lingo of watch-keeping.

re-scrub   'Do it over again.' To repeat a performance that has not rendered approval—such as an evolution in general drill; also to be given a re-examination in any subject. *Etymology*: When a mess has not been scrubbed out to the divisional officer's satisfaction he may order a 're-scrub'—a punitive evolution, to be performed in the dinner hour.

rind   Synonymous with **hide** and **skin**.

rock scorpion   A term of contempt accorded to anyone of raw experience or mediocre ability. Native dockyard workers of Gibraltar and other Spaniards who served in the British Navy on that station were known as rock scorpions, though they had nothing in common with the arachnids reputed to infest the famous Rock.

Rocky   A Royal Naval or Fleet Reserve man.

rook   Refers to the mess; the 'at home' of a naval man. Synonymous with **cottage, domicile** and **drum**.

round the buoy   To go 'around the buoy' implies a second helping at meals; to go 'around the buoy three times' means partaking of four platefuls. From the lingo of boat-racing.

round up   To 'round up' a person is to dispatch a number of men to find him without delay.

Royal   The orthodox (and respectful) manner of addressing any Royal Marine when his name is not known.

rub   Blame, the responsibility (see **stand the rub**); also a loan, e.g. 'Give us a rub of your pencil?' It is associated with the old custom of borrowing a dip or a 'rub' from a shipmate's tin of polishing paste, or **scourers**.

rubber   A loan; a corruption of '**rub** of', e.g. 'What about a rubber?' 'A rubber what?' 'A rub of a quid.'

rub up   Instruction in any subject; to study diligently.

rum-fiend   As the term implies, a man who is a glutton for rum; also the hard-featured toper [heavy drinker] who presides at the **fanny** and serves out **shaky** tots in order to insure more **plussers** for himself. See also **shaky**.

runner   A messenger; the comm's 'runner' is the commander's messenger.

run out to a clinch   A state of acute bankruptcy. A ship is 'run out to a clinch' when she cannot pay out any more cable.

run round   Instructions in any subject which necessitate movement from one department to another. For instance, a young officer may ask a turret sweeper for a 'run round' the gunhouse. This would involve an excursion around, above and below the guns, at which the tyro would learn many of the mysteries of hydraulic or electrical machinery as well as the somewhat complicated wonders of the director firing apparatus.

S

sail close to the wind Another expression that has reached the vocabulary of Fleet Street. To run neck and neck with disaster; to all but ask for trouble. A craft that sails close to the wind is, of course, in grave danger of being capsized.

Sails Nickname for the sailmaker.

salt beef squire Synonymous with **sand king**.

salvo A pat retort. A rejoinder so dynamic as to **sink** an opponent. *Etymology*: A salvo is a number of guns fired simultaneously. Synonymous with **broadside**.

sand king A boatswain. The senior boatswain of the ship is nicknamed 'Tommy'—never 'Tommy Pipes', as many civilians think. Synonymous with **salt beef squire**.

scale Commensurate punishment by forfeiture of wages and stoppage of leave for a delinquent who has been absent without leave. The scale runs: For every three hours' absence a man loses a day's pay and leave; for thirty-six hours' absence the loss would be twelve days' pay and stoppage of leave.

scaly back A veteran; one who has been too long in the Navy.

scats Synonymous with **tin-hats**, **blitzed**, **canned**, **half-rats**, **shot away**, **well oiled**, etc.

Schoolie The nickname for the ship's schoolmaster, who, by the way, is a warrant officer. In small ships, however, the status of acting-schoolmaster is often conferred on some brainy rating who is particularly brilliant at mathematics. Very often an A.B. takes on acting-schoolmaster and ship's librarian, for which he receives the stupendous emolument of eightpence a day.

Scotland Yard Synonymous with **Crushers** and **Gestapo**.

scourers A polishing paste composed of granulated brick dust and oil. Our forefathers had to be content with this crude compound to get their brightwork cleaned.

Scouse Nickname for a Liverpool man or anyone who sports a marked Liverpool accent.

scout A troublesome fellow; a schemer; one who skates off when any work is indicated. Synonymous with **skate**. See also **bird**, **crow**, **fowl** and **pelican**.

scran bag The lost property office of the Royal Navy. It is usually a cell into which all clothing left lying about (an untidy transgression) and all unclaimed belongings are dumped. The tax imposed for the redemption of each piece of clothing or article is one square-inch of soap.

screw down To defeat; the analogy is an exaggeration, in that it implies screwing down the lid of one's coffin.

Scribe Once a poetic manner of addressing the ship's writer.

sculling In the neighbourhood, imminent. 'Look out, the comm is sculling' is a warning that that the mighty potentate is not far away.

sculling about To leave anything 'sculling about' is to leave it carelessly unguarded to the mercy of a regime that frowns upon all slovenliness; in other words, one is liable to lose the article.

scun; scun to the wide   An acute state of bankruptcy. Scun—believed to be the past participle of 'skinned'.

scurs   A badly grown **set** of whiskers in its early stages. Also the inelegant nickname bestowed on the owner of the scurs.

sea lawyer   This complimentary term usually applies to one who is famed for his knowledge of King's Rules and Regulations and Admiralty Instructions, or to one well acquainted with naval history and political and social aspects of naval life in general. His judgement is generally appealed to when arguments break out.

sea-legs   A man is not considered to have 'shipped his sea-legs' until he can comfortably maintain his equilibrium in defiance of the rolling and pitching of the ship.

seaman gunner's wash   A hurried toilet with shaving-brush and water after shaving. In the old gunnery ship H.M.S. *Cambridge* the daily shave was a very strict order, and the merest suspicion of down on the visage when liberty men were being inspected precluded a poor matloe from going ashore. Soon after gunnery classes dispersed, liberty men fell in. In the meantime, many hurried shaves and improvised washes were performed to ensure passing inspection and **catching the boat**.

second dickey   A species of assistant manager. When two men are appointed to the same job, the junior of the two is called the 'second dickey'.

set   A beard; a set of whiskers—or **scurs**.

seven-beller   Having a meal at half-past three in the afternoon—seven bells.

shaky   Backward, inefficient, incompetent, unhealthy, insalubrious, incomplete. A sick man is often described as looking 'pretty shaky'. A man may be shaky at certain drills or subjects. Again when a man's leave is approaching termination his shipmates say: 'His leave is looking shaky now.' The term also applies to insufficiency. 'A shaky tot', for instance, implies a very stingy measure. The idiom here is the genesis of the colourless adjective traced to that very selfish and unpopular figure, the **rum-fiend**, whose hand shakes noticeably when he measures out his messmates' rum.

shark   To steal.

sharp around the bows   Sharp-featured. A man is usually told he is looking 'sharp around the bows' after he has had a haircut.

sharp end   A facetious reference to the bows or fore-castle of the ship. Likewise, the quarter-deck or stern is termed the 'blunt end'.

shifting backstay   Applies to a rating who is being constantly shifted from one job to another. It is an equitable term and is usually attributable to a rating whose own job is so mediocre that he is usually sent off to fill every temporary vacancy of more importance.

shipshape   Trim, orderly, neat.

Shorty   Nickname for a diminutive person.

shot away   Synonymous with **tin-hats, blitzed, canned, half-rats, scats, well oiled,** etc.

shovel engineer   Old name for **dustman**. Synonymous with **clinker-knocker** and **fireman**.

show a leg   To this day, when calling the hands, every morning the boatswain's mate exhorts the sleepers to 'show a leg'—note: not 'shake a leg'. In the old days, when women slept in hammocks on board, the boatswain's mate wanted to ensure that no rating retained the warmth of his hammock by pretending to be a woman. His order therefore that everybody should 'show a leg' helped to assure him of the sex of the owner of each foot. A woman usually sported a neat and dainty ankle, while a matloe's hoof (especially in those remote days) fell very much short of the picturesque.

sink   To defeat in an argument.

skate   Synonymous with **scout**. See also **bird, crow, fowl** and **pelican**.

skin   Signifies nerve, impassivity, brazenness. Synonymous with **hide** and **rind**.

Skipper   Needless to say, the captain (who is never the **Old Man** (ii) in the Navy), but mention here has been given to explain the possessive case—

Skipper's   Simply that and nothing more, but it means such a lot. It is really captain's report. When a delinquent's transgression is much too serious for the commander to deal with, he passes the case on for investigation by the captain in exactly the same way as a magistrate commits a man for trial. One might say, 'If Smithy gets Skipper's for coming aboard **tin-hats**, he can bid a fond farewell to one of his badges.'

Sky   The nickname for all Turners. It was once the monopoly of seamen of marked efficiency aloft; later it applied to all ratings whose swaggering gait was characteristic of the old-time sailor. The term hails from 'sky sail', the uppermost sail on the mast.

Sloshy   Outdated term for **Chef**. Synonymous with **Greasy-Neck**.

Smile Awhile   Synonymous with **Acid Drops**, **Aggs (Agony Column)**, **Bitter Weed**, **Caustic**, **Clanking Irons** and **Famous Crimes**.

Smoke   London is affectionately termed 'the Smoke'.

Snaky   The appellative of all who are excessively slender.

soft soap   Praise given tactfully in order to encourage a higher standard of efficiency—that it might be fulfilled that 'the more you do in this **hooker**, the more they want you to do.'

soldier on   To complete a period of service in the Navy. The term usually applies to an offender who has served a term of imprisonment in a naval prison but has not been dismissed from the Service at its completion.

Sparko; Sparks   Any member of the wireless branch.

Spithead pheasant   New name for a kipper.

split yarn   When anything is in complete readiness for the immediate execution of a job it is referred to as being 'on a split yarn'. When a delinquent's offence is liable to cause the loss of his good-conduct badge, that badge is said to be 'looking **shaky**' or 'hanging on a split yarn'. The analogy is from drills where wires, all in readiness, are secured to anything adjacent with a very small yarn that will hold temporarily, but with the drill commencing, one good tug sets the wire clear and the drill goes on briskly.

Stalin   As a compliment to the strongman of Russia, a man called Joe in 1940 may have found himself called 'Stalin' in 1943.

stand easy   Otherwise breakfast. 'What are we on for stand easy?' means 'What do we eat for breakfast?' Breakfast time was once so short (about twenty minutes' duration) that a rating had to be particularly swift if he wished to enjoy a smoke in addition ('catch the smoke boat', as it was called). The alternative was having to wait until 10.30 a.m., when 'Stand easy' was piped. This was a respite of ten minutes for the purpose of smoking—as it was death to the law to be caught smoking in service time in those days. In later days, the breakfast time was lengthened and the 10.30 stand easy abolished. As the hands were then permitted to smoke only in the breakfast hour, the whole period became identified with 'stand easy'.

stand the rub   To shoulder the blame for any contingency. See also **take the can back**.

steam   To expedite matters; to hasten.

stokehold boatswain   Another species of slang that is dying out—a warrant engineer. Synonymous with **tiffy boatswain**.

stone frigate   Generally applies to a naval barracks. The term is seldom heard to-day.

Storm-trooper Before the Second World War the term applied to a short-service man, and the manner in which a number of them made a headlong dive at mealtimes earned for them this obstreperous nickname.

strafe To scold; from the kultured lingo—God bless the mark.

stretch it To break leave. Before 1914, naval ratings were far more gregarious than they are these days; while on liberty, as many as a dozen comrades at a time kept loyally together. After a Bacchanalian 'night before', the suggestion from one sore-headed reveller to 'stretch it' was often carried by vote.

Stripey Nickname for a sergeant of marines. Also any able seaman sporting three good-conduct badges is hailed familiarly as 'Stripey'.

strongers The mixture of hot water and such chemicals as caustic, soft soap and powder for removing dirty stains and, in general, simplifying the great labour of cleansing.

sub Otherwise substitute; to take another man's place; to perform another man's duty. A man who is watch on board may, if of good character, get ashore provided he finds a sub from the watch ashore willing to do his duty. That sub would then be obliged to undertake all his duties.

Subby Nickname for a sub-lieutenant. He is usually spoken of and often addressed as 'Subby'.

Swain The coxswain of a destroyer or submarine.

sweeper A general cleaner and caretaker of any decks, department or store-room on board ship.

Swift Often a derisive misnomer applied to one who is notoriously slow of movement.

swing To cancel.

swinging the lead Has diverse meanings. A prudent delay pending a decision; skulking; loitering; a man who dodges paying for a round of drinks after he him-self has been liberally treated is said to 'swing the lead'. *Etymology*: The duty of the leadsman in the chains is to keep on heaving the lead—the proximity of shallow water being suspected. As it is, however, a laborious and tiring ordeal, he elects to have a rest by keeping the leadline still and therefore perpendicular. Immediately the officer of the watch or navigator heaves in sight his attitude changes to pretentious activity, and he starts swinging his leadline. Instead of swinging the lead over his head, however, he waits until authority disappears and then comes to rest once more.

swinging round the buoy   A person who clings to a soft job in order to dodge going to sea is said to 'swing around the buoy'—which, of course, is what a ship does in the welcome security of harbour. Dockyard employees who manoeuvred to dodge being sent to Scotland or abroad have been accused by their more loyal co-workers of 'swinging round the buoy'.

T

take on   To 'take on' means that after having served twelve years' active service (commonly alluded to as 'first twelve') a man re-engages for a further ten years' service in order to qualify for a life pension.

take the can back   To stand the blame for anything or to be the only one of a party to whom it falls the lot to perform a task that must be done. In the general mess (or **Jago**'s) each table was supplied with dishes of meat, greens, potatoes, etc. from which each diner helped himself. Often some hungry trencherman was confronted with an empty tin-dish and perforce considered himself very unfortunate, as he was obliged to take the tin-dish (can) back to the galley to have it replenished—after which others came along and helped themselves. See also **stand the rub**.

tally   A name. 'What's your tally?'

Tanky The potentate who attends to the fresh-water tanks. Officially he is called the 'captain of the hold' and he works with the supply staff. He is a conspicuous figure at the grog tub, to which he brings the necessary water for diluting the rum.

tap (i) To negotiate quietly, secretly or tactfully for a loan or a favour; to find out how much one possesses by a tentative whisper, e.g. 'I tapped him for half-a-quid.' The analogy is tapping a barrel in order to estimate the amount of liquor it holds.

(ii) To do a tap, toot, moan, howl, weep or bar, otherwise to 'have a weed on', is to complain, to find fault or lament.

Tarzan Synonymous with **Chimp** and **Doggo**.

taut hand A good fighting-man; one who can hold his own in a melee. Synonymous with **good hand**.

ticket A certificate indicating that a man's services are no longer required. A rating is said to 'get his ticket' when discharged from the Navy (sometimes described as 'put on the beach') whether through being (a) medically unfit, (b) incompetent, or (c) that his character does not approach the requisite moral standard.

'Ticket' is believed to be sinisterly confounded with ticket-of-leave.

tickler A cigarette made from the tinned tobacco supplied to the Navy. Also (and originally) a short-service man. *Etymology*: The short-service system was introduced into the Navy by Lord Selborne in 1903—about the same time as Tickler's jam became an accepted ration in the Royal Navy. [Lord Selborne was William Waldegrave Palmer, 2nd Earl of Selborne (17 October 1859–26 February 1942), who served as the first Lord of the Admiralty from 1900 to 1905.]

tiddley Neat, tidy.

tied up Married. 'I can't afford to run ashore very much since I've been tied up.' Authors and pressmen please note: naval men never say 'spliced' in relation to marriage.

tiffy Short for 'artificer'; an engine room artificer (E.R.A.)

tiffy boatswain Synonymous with **stokehold boatswain**.

Tin-eye   Nickname given to anyone who sports a monocle.

Tin-fish   Torpedoes.

tin-hats   Figure of speech which applies to one who has had a good cargo of alcohol. In ancient days in some English prisons people brought in in an advanced state of intoxication were compelled to wear a sort of iron helmet which guarded against serious head injuries in the event of their casting loose and banging their craniums against the cell walls. Thus 'tin-hat'. Synonymous with **blitzed, canned, half rats, scats, shot away, well oiled**, etc.

tin man   To come the 'tin man' or 'on the tin man' means to take great liberties, exceed one's duties or to assume a bombastic authority that is beyond one's prerogative to exercise. Believed to be analogous with the original iron (tin) target shaped as a man which figured at rifle ranges. This metallic figure sprang up into view only to disappear again before the tyro had time to come on aim. This act of springing up was associated with audacious bounce; all very well in a target, but not quite tolerable in society. See also **old soldier**.

tin-pot Ordinary; common or garden; mediocre. The term implies cheapness.

toe-rag Salt fish.

Tommy Nickname of the senior boatswain. From 'Tommy Pipes' of the ancient Navy, but Pipes is never mentioned in these enlightened days. See also **salt beef squire** and **sand king**.

too late in the commish A taunt at the useless efforts to bring about certain changes which promise no great benefit or advantage. *Etymology*: Certain promotions usually took place when a slip was paid off, but all these had been booked some months before. Therefore, towards the close of the commission, efforts to catch Authority's eye by a marked display of diligence were greeted with the ironic reminder that it was 'too late in the commish'.

top-heavy Another synonym for drunk. A ship is said to be top-heavy when her masts, rigging or upper structure are extra-heavy, therefore causing her to roll a good deal.

top line To be 'on the top line' signifies readiness, punctuality, or to be on the spot to seize the most favourable

112

opportunity. On a 'wash clothes' night' in the Victorian Navy, three clothes-lines stretched fore and aft the upper deck on one or both sides. They were so rigged that when triced up the washing presented a sloped spectacle; the inboard line was the highest, the centre line a little lower, and the outboard line lower still. Washing hung on the top (or upper) line had the most favourable chance of drying as it was higher in the air and free from obscuration by the others. Consequently, matloes were very eager to finish **dobeying** in time so that they might hang it on the top line.

top of the tree   Refers to the highest in authority. A matloe's avowal that he will go to the 'top of the tree' may mean laying a grievance before the admiral of his squadron or even getting in touch with the First Lord of the Admiralty.

top-piece   Of blessed memory: the allowance of fresh meat which a rating on the provision list was allowed to take ashore once a week. It was usually a cut of anything up to four pounds of the finest prime beef.

touch it light   A prudent reminder to be abstemious in the consumption of 'eats' or 'drinks', as when handing a shipmate a cup of rum and asking him to 'touch it light': this is a tactful request not to take too deep a draught. 'Touch the spuds light, lads,' the caterer of a mess dutifully warns his messmates to exercise economy in taking potatoes so that all may have a share.

towny People who hail from the same town or city regard themselves as 'townies' of one another. Because of their loyalty to the old homestead they usually fraternise, but such a proceeding has often proved to be a very unwise policy. There are many strong friendships in the Royal Navy, but seldom does a genuine David and Jonathan or a Damon and Pythias hail from the same town. Naval proverb: Don't let 'townies' know all your business if you don't want all the town to know it.

treacle; treacle factory A training-ship or establishment. In the Victorian era, treacle was one of the luxuries given to training-ship boys. The name has stuck. Although there has been no treacle issued as a ration during the 20th century, any man recalling his old training-ship will refer to her as 'the Treacle'.

troop To troop anybody is to take him in front of the officer of the watch as a defaulter.

Troops, The   The proletariat of the lower deck. All ratings dressed as seamen below the rank of leading seaman.

Trunky   Synonymous with **Conky**.

tub   To puzzle, to perplex.

Tubby   The sobriquet of anyone who is corpulent. From a tub—rather round.

tuck a strand   Ingratiating tactful manoeuvre to win favour. When one tucks the first strand in splicing wire one gets an important part of the work done.

Turkey   Any member of the Royal Marines. 'Turkey' recalls the once bright-red tunic that Royal Marines wore. Synonymous with **Bullock** and **Leatherneck**.

Turko   A nickname usually accorded to a libertine, a roué.

U

U Boat   An uncharitable jibe meted out to anyone inclined to be round-shouldered.

upper   Short for upper deck. 'Are you coming on the upper?'

up the line   Usually refers to the dear old homestead when it means a railway journey away from the home port. A person is said to be 'up the line' when through absent-mindedness or preoccupation he does his work inaccurately. The implication is that his thoughts are with the folks at home and not on his work.

up the Straits   Pertaining to that once very expensive but now rather tumultuous region, the Mediterranean. As a naval station it extends from Vigo even as far as Constantinople. Some years ago no rating was considered staid or experienced unless he had 'done the Straits'.

us This plural pronoun is usually identified with 'our ship', as e.g. ''Tis **Callao** aboard of us.' Again the expression 'We had a bloke in us' implies that the speaker refers to an old shipmate who had served with him on some other ship.

W

wall-flower   Scathing reference to any ship which remains moored to a dockyard wall for a prolonged period.

wangle   To solicit; to secure a favour by diplomatic means; to borrow. 'I'll have to try and wangle five bob somewhere.'

wash-deck   Generally means ordinary and mediocre as connected with the Service. The wash-deck boatswain was the junior boatswain of a big ship who mainly supervised the cleaning of the upper deck (hence **sand king**) and did not share the responsibilities of the senior or commissioned boatswain. A naval rating who contributes to a journal or is famed for some literary ability may be referred to as a 'wash-deck journalist'.

water-rat   Of shameful memory. The 'water-rats' were a very unpopular branch of the London Metropolitan Police employed at naval ports. Their main duties were to **round up** all naval absentees and escort them back to their ships. At eight every morning they were very busy visiting pubs, clubs and lodging-houses where sailors congregated. They were very keen on arresting their victims because they received a whole pound for each culprit. Needless to say, the emolument came out of the unfortunate absentee's slender income. The Royal Navy severed all connection with this infamous clique round about 1913.

well oiled   Synonymous with **tin-hats, blitzed, canned, half-rats, scats, shot away,** etc.

Westo   West-country attributes; may apply to anyone in the western wing of the Navy—Devonport division. 'Westo' is usually associated with a stinginess of disposition: if a man is said to be 'proper Westo' he is considered mean and niggardly, as many Cornishmen have an undeserved reputation for parsimony. An east-country mariner may say 'he is a **Duffo**,' i.e. he is west-country division. The **Duffo** springs from the west-countryman's reputed partiality for plum-duff.

wet   (i) A drink of any liquid.
      (ii) Caption of Life's misfits; the tragic label of the inefficient; a condition of mental instability which may

be due to imprudence, eccentricity, incompetence or insanity. Synonymous with **batchy** (i), **crackers** and **loopy**.

wet at the boathoist   'He's had a wet at the boathoist': a term of contempt directed at the pot-valiant individual who comes on board affecting to be the worse for liquor. As liberty men are inspected on arrival on board, it is obvious one cannot be very drunk after passing under the eye of the officer of the watch. Leaving the quarter-deck, liberty men, before coming forward, usually passed the boathoist where, it was often satirically assumed, revellers adjourn to have a final and most devastating libation.

wet it up   To celebrate by a drinking bout.

whack   A section; a ration.

white rat   A crawling sycophant in human shape who aims to advance his prospects by carrying tales.

windward   'To get to windward' implies gain, profit in any transaction or achieving the advantage over others. (Obversely, 'to go to leeward' signifies loss or misfortune. See **lose deal**.)

windy   Nervous, bewildered. From 'get the wind up'.

winged   Caught in the act; apprehended.

winger   A protégé. See **Old Man** (i).

work ticket   A man is said to 'work his ticket' when he essays to gain his discharge from the Navy on medical grounds. Mental instability: being a very cogent avenue under this heading, a man who does something very silly or indiscreet is hailed with the rebuke that he is 'working his ticket'.

Y

Yank Not necessarily an American: any matloe who apes a nasal twang or a cowboy swagger will very speedily earn the name of 'Yank'.